My Ireland Bucket List

This Adventure Journal Belongs To:

_____

Places I May Want To Visit

_____ The Lakes of Killarney

_____ The Ring Of Kerry

_____ The Cliffs of Moher

_____ Newgrange, Knowth and Dowth

_____ Dublin City

_____ The Giant's Causeway

_____ Hill of Tara

_____ Knocknarea in Sligo

_____ Blarney Castle and Blarney Stone

_____ The Burren

_____ Glendalough

_____ Bunratty Castle

_____ Dingle Peninsula

_____ Kylemore Abbey

_____ Titanic Shipyard in Belfast

_____ Connemara National Park

_____ Skellig Michael Island

_____ English Market

_____ The Rock of Cashel

_____ Kinsale

_____ Slieve League

_____ The Long Room Library at Trinity

_____ College

_____ Irish Sky Garden

_____ Dunmore Cave

Places I May Want To Visit

- _____ Newgrange
- _____ St. Michan's Mummies
- _____ Kilmainham Gaol
- _____ Sean's Bar
- _____ The Hungry Tree
- _____ Jerpoint Abbey
- _____ National Leprechaun Museum
- _____ Saint Audoen's Gate
- _____ Kyteler's Inn
- _____ National Museum of Ireland
- _____ The Wonderful Barn
- _____ Abandoned Menlo Castle
- _____ Doolin Cave
- _____ Charleville Castle
- _____ Old Red Iron Bridge
- _____ St. Patrick's Purgatory
- _____ The Hole of the Sorrows
- _____ The Little Museum of Dublin
- _____ Sweny's Pharmacy
- _____ Kilmacduagh Round Tower
- _____ Great Blasket Island
- _____ Birr Castle Box Hedge
- _____ Boyeeghter Bay
- _____ MV Plassy
- _____ Rindoon

Places I May Want To Visit

_____ Freemasons' Hall
_____ The Irish National Famine Museum
_____ Brigit's Celtic Garden
_____ Kinnitty Pyramid
_____ Leviathon of Parsonstown
_____ Kells Priory
_____ Rathcroghan
_____ Bridges of Ross
_____ Irish Jewish Museum
_____ Saint Brendan's Well
_____ Foynes Flying Boat Museum
_____ The Oscar Wilde House
_____ Hore Abbey
_____ John Kavanagh Pub
_____ Secret Celtic Tree Cross
_____ Fort Dunree
_____ Boole House
_____ Samuel Beckett Bridge
_____ Writers' Room at Wicklow Heather
_____ Irish National Stud and Gardens
_____ Benbulben Barite Mine
_____ Oratory of the Sacred Heart
_____ Castleboro House
_____ Kilbeggan Distillery
_____ Great Blasket Island

Places I May Want To Visit

___   _____

___   _____

___   _____

___   _____

___   _____

___   _____

___   _____

___   _____

___   _____

___   _____

___   _____

___   _____

___   _____

___   _____

___   _____

___   _____

___   _____

___   _____

___   _____

___   _____

Places I May Want To Visit

___   _____

___   _____

___   _____

___   _____

___   _____

___   _____

___   _____

___   _____

___   _____

___   _____

___   _____

___   _____

___   _____

___   _____

___   _____

___   _____

___   _____

___   _____

___   _____

___   _____

___   _____

___   _____

___   _____

___   _____

1 Noteworthy

Ireland Bucket List Item

1

Attraction: _____

Location: _____

Why I Want To Visit Here: _____

_____

_____

────── *The Adventure Begins* ──────

Date Of Visit: _____

My Experience: _____

_____

_____

_____

_____

_____

_____

What I Enjoyed Most: _____

_____

_____

The People I Met: _____

_____

_____

2 Noteworthy

Ireland Bucket List Item

2

Attraction: _____

Location: _____

Why I Want To Visit Here: _____

_____

_____

———— *The Adventure Begins* ————

Date Of Visit: _____

My Experience: _____

_____

_____

_____

_____

_____

What I Enjoyed Most: _____

_____

_____

The People I Met: _____

_____

_____

3 Noteworthy

Ireland Bucket List Item

3

Attraction: _____

Location: _____

Why I Want To Visit Here: _____

_____

_____

———— *The Adventure Begins* ————

Date Of Visit: _____

My Experience: _____

_____

_____

_____

_____

_____

What I Enjoyed Most: _____

_____

_____

The People I Met: _____

_____

_____

4

Noteworthy

Ireland Bucket List Item

Attraction: _____

Location: _____

Why I Want To Visit Here: _____

_____

_____

———— *The Adventure Begins* ————

Date Of Visit: _____

My Experience: _____

_____

_____

_____

_____

_____

What I Enjoyed Most: _____

_____

_____

The People I Met: _____

_____

_____

5 Noteworthy

Ireland Bucket List Item 5

Attraction: _____

Location: _____

Why I Want To Visit Here: _____

_____

_____

———— *The Adventure Begins* ————

Date Of Visit: _____

My Experience: _____

_____

_____

_____

_____

_____

What I Enjoyed Most: _____

_____

_____

The People I Met: _____

_____

_____

6 Noteworthy

Ireland Bucket List Item

Attraction: _____

Location: _____

Why I Want To Visit Here: _____

. _____

_____

―――― *The Adventure Begins* ――――――――

Date Of Visit: _____

My Experience: _____

_____

_____

_____

_____

_____

_____

What I Enjoyed Most: _____

_____

_____

The People I Met: _____

_____

_____

7 Noteworthy

Ireland Bucket List Item

7

Attraction: _____

Location: _____

Why I Want To Visit Here: _____

_____

_____

──── *The Adventure Begins* ─────────────

Date Of Visit: _____

My Experience: _____

_____

_____

_____

_____

_____

What I Enjoyed Most: _____

_____

_____

The People I Met: _____

_____

_____

8

Noteworthy

Ireland Bucket List Item

8

Attraction: _____

Location: _____

Why I Want To Visit Here: _____

_____

_____

———*The Adventure Begins*————————

Date Of Visit: _____

My Experience: _____

_____

_____

_____

_____

_____

_____

What I Enjoyed Most: _____

_____

_____

The People I Met: _____

_____

_____

9 Noteworthy

Ireland Bucket List Item

Attraction: _____

Location: _____

Why I Want To Visit Here: _____

_____

_____

───── *The Adventure Begins* ─────

Date Of Visit: _____

My Experience: _____

_____

_____

_____

_____

_____

What I Enjoyed Most: _____

_____

_____

The People I Met: _____

_____

_____

10

Noteworthy

Ireland Bucket List Item 10

Attraction: _____

Location: _____

Why I Want To Visit Here: _____

_____

_____

———— *The Adventure Begins* ————

Date Of Visit: _____

My Experience: _____

_____

_____

_____

_____

_____

What I Enjoyed Most: _____

_____

_____

The People I Met: _____

_____

_____

11

Noteworthy

Ireland Bucket List Item 11

Attraction: _____

Location: _____

Why I Want To Visit Here: _____

_____

_____

───── *The Adventure Begins* ─────

Date Of Visit: _____

My Experience: _____

_____

_____

_____

_____

_____

What I Enjoyed Most: _____

_____

_____

The People I Met: _____

_____

_____

12

Noteworthy

Ireland Bucket List Item 12

Attraction: _____

Location: _____

Why I Want To Visit Here: _____

_____

_____

———— *The Adventure Begins* ————

Date Of Visit: _____

My Experience: _____

_____

_____

_____

_____

_____

What I Enjoyed Most: _____

_____

_____

The People I Met: _____

_____

_____

13

Ireland Bucket List Item 13

Attraction: _____

Location: _____

Why I Want To Visit Here: _____

_____

_____

—————— *The Adventure Begins* ——————

Date Of Visit: _____

My Experience: _____

_____

_____

_____

_____

_____

What I Enjoyed Most: _____

_____

_____

The People I Met: _____

_____

_____

14

Ireland Bucket List Item 14

Attraction: _____

Location: _____

Why I Want To Visit Here: _____

_____

_____

───── *The Adventure Begins* ──────────

Date Of Visit: _____

My Experience: _____

_____

_____

_____

_____

_____

What I Enjoyed Most: _____

_____

_____

The People I Met: _____

_____

_____

15 Noteworthy

Ireland Bucket List Item 15

Attraction: _____

Location: _____

Why I Want To Visit Here: _____

_____

_____

——— *The Adventure Begins* ———

Date Of Visit: _____

My Experience: _____

_____

_____

_____

_____

_____

What I Enjoyed Most: _____

_____

_____

The People I Met: _____

_____

_____

16 Noteworthy

Ireland Bucket List Item 16

Attraction: _____

Location: _____

Why I Want To Visit Here: _____

_____

_____

———— *The Adventure Begins* ————————

Date Of Visit: _____

My Experience: _____

_____

_____

_____

_____

_____

What I Enjoyed Most: _____

_____

_____

The People I Met: _____

_____

_____

17 Noteworthy

Ireland Bucket List Item 17

Attraction: _____

Location: _____

Why I Want To Visit Here: _____

_____

_____

────── *The Adventure Begins* ──────

Date Of Visit: _____

My Experience: _____

_____

_____

_____

_____

_____

What I Enjoyed Most: _____

_____

_____

The People I Met: _____

_____

_____

18

Noteworthy

Ireland Bucket List Item 18

Attraction: _____

Location: _____

Why I Want To Visit Here: _____

_____

_____

———— *The Adventure Begins* ————

Date Of Visit: _____

My Experience: _____

_____

_____

_____

_____

_____

_____

What I Enjoyed Most: _____

_____

_____

The People I Met: _____

_____

_____

19

Ireland Bucket List Item 19

Attraction: _____

Location: _____

Why I Want To Visit Here: _____

_____

_____

———— *The Adventure Begins* ————————

Date Of Visit: _____

My Experience: _____

_____

_____

_____

_____

_____

What I Enjoyed Most: _____

_____

_____

The People I Met: _____

_____

_____

20 Noteworthy

Ireland Bucket List Item 20

Attraction: _____

Location: _____

Why I Want To Visit Here: _____

_____

_____

———— *The Adventure Begins* ————

Date Of Visit: _____

My Experience: _____

_____

_____

_____

_____

_____

What I Enjoyed Most: _____

_____

_____

The People I Met: _____

_____

_____

21

Noteworthy

Ireland Bucket List Item 21

Attraction: _____

Location: _____

Why I Want To Visit Here: _____

_____

_____

———— *The Adventure Begins* ————

Date Of Visit: _____

My Experience: _____

_____

_____

_____

_____

_____

What I Enjoyed Most: _____

_____

_____

The People I Met: _____

_____

_____

Noteworthy

Ireland Bucket List Item 22

Attraction: _____

Location: _____

Why I Want To Visit Here: _____

_____

_____

————— *The Adventure Begins* —————

Date Of Visit: _____

My Experience: _____

_____

_____

_____

_____

_____

_____

What I Enjoyed Most: _____

_____

_____

The People I Met: _____

_____

_____

23 Noteworthy

Ireland Bucket List Item 23

Attraction: _____

Location: _____

Why I Want To Visit Here: _____

_____

_____

──── *The Adventure Begins* ────

Date Of Visit: _____

My Experience: _____

_____

_____

_____

_____

_____

_____

What I Enjoyed Most: _____

_____

_____

The People I Met: _____

_____

_____

24 Noteworthy

Ireland Bucket List Item 24

Attraction: _____

Location: _____

Why I Want To Visit Here: _____

_____

_____

——— *The Adventure Begins* ———————

Date Of Visit: _____

My Experience: _____

_____

_____

_____

_____

_____

What I Enjoyed Most: _____

_____

_____

The People I Met: _____

_____

_____

25

Noteworthy

Ireland Bucket List Item 25

Attraction: _____

Location: _____

Why I Want To Visit Here: _____

_____

_____

───── *The Adventure Begins* ─────

Date Of Visit: _____

My Experience: _____

_____

_____

_____

_____

_____

What I Enjoyed Most: _____

_____

_____

_____

The People I Met: _____

_____

_____

26

Noteworthy

Ireland Bucket List Item 26

Attraction: _____

Location: _____

Why I Want To Visit Here: _____

_____

_____

———— *The Adventure Begins* ————————

Date Of Visit: _____

My Experience: _____

_____

_____

_____

_____

_____

What I Enjoyed Most: _____

_____

_____

The People I Met: _____

_____

_____

27

Noteworthy

Ireland Bucket List Item 27

Attraction: _____

Location: _____

Why I Want To Visit Here: _____

_____

_____

———— *The Adventure Begins* ————

Date Of Visit: _____

My Experience: _____

_____

_____

_____

_____

_____

What I Enjoyed Most: _____

_____

_____

The People I Met: _____

_____

_____

28

Ireland Bucket List Item 28

Attraction: _____

Location: _____

Why I Want To Visit Here: _____

_____

_____

—— *The Adventure Begins* ——————————

Date Of Visit: _____

My Experience: _____

_____

_____

_____

_____

_____

What I Enjoyed Most: _____

_____

_____

The People I Met: _____

_____

_____

29

Noteworthy

Ireland Bucket List Item **29**

Attraction: _____

Location: _____

Why I Want To Visit Here: _____

_____

_____

——— *The Adventure Begins* ———

Date Of Visit: _____

My Experience: _____

_____

_____

_____

_____

_____

_____

What I Enjoyed Most: _____

_____

_____

_____

The People I Met: _____

_____

_____

30

Ireland Bucket List Item 30

Attraction: _____

Location: _____

Why I Want To Visit Here: _____

_____

_____

———— *The Adventure Begins* ————————

Date Of Visit: _____

My Experience: _____

_____

_____

_____

_____

_____

What I Enjoyed Most: _____

_____

_____

The People I Met: _____

_____

_____

31

Ireland Bucket List Item 31

Attraction: _____

Location: _____

Why I Want To Visit Here: _____

_____

_____

——— *The Adventure Begins* ———————

Date Of Visit: _____

My Experience: _____

_____

_____

_____

_____

_____

_____

What I Enjoyed Most: _____

_____

_____

The People I Met: _____

_____

_____

32

Noteworthy

Ireland Bucket List Item 32

Attraction: _____

Location: _____

Why I Want To Visit Here: _____

_____

_____

―――― *The Adventure Begins* ――――

Date Of Visit: _____

My Experience: _____

_____

_____

_____

_____

_____

What I Enjoyed Most: _____

_____

_____

The People I Met: _____

_____

_____

Ireland Bucket List Item 33

Attraction: _____

Location: _____

Why I Want To Visit Here: _____

_____

_____

——— *The Adventure Begins* ———

Date Of Visit: _____

My Experience: _____

_____

_____

_____

_____

_____

What I Enjoyed Most: _____

_____

_____

The People I Met: _____

_____

_____

34

Ireland Bucket List Item **34**

Attraction: _____

Location: _____

Why I Want To Visit Here: _____

_____

_____

────── *The Adventure Begins* ──────

Date Of Visit: _____

My Experience: _____

_____

_____

_____

_____

_____

What I Enjoyed Most: _____

_____

_____

The People I Met: _____

_____

_____

35

Noteworthy

Ireland Bucket List Item 35

Attraction: _____

Location: _____

Why I Want To Visit Here: _____

_____

_____

──── *The Adventure Begins* ─────────

Date Of Visit: _____

My Experience: _____

_____

_____

_____

_____

_____

What I Enjoyed Most: _____

_____

_____

The People I Met: _____

_____

_____

36

Noteworthy

Ireland Bucket List Item 36

Attraction: _____

Location: _____

Why I Want To Visit Here: _____

_____

_____

──── *The Adventure Begins* ─────────────

Date Of Visit: _____

My Experience: _____

_____

_____

_____

_____

_____

What I Enjoyed Most: _____

_____

_____

The People I Met: _____

_____

_____

37

Ireland Bucket List Item 37

Attraction: _____

Location: _____

Why I Want To Visit Here: _____

_____

_____

────── *The Adventure Begins* ──────────

Date Of Visit: _____

My Experience: _____

_____

_____

_____

_____

_____

What I Enjoyed Most: _____

_____

_____

The People I Met: _____

_____

_____

38

Noteworthy

Ireland Bucket List Item 38

Attraction: _____

Location: _____

Why I Want To Visit Here: _____

_____

_____

────── *The Adventure Begins* ──────────

Date Of Visit: _____

My Experience: _____

_____

_____

_____

_____

_____

What I Enjoyed Most: _____

_____

_____

The People I Met: _____

_____

_____

39

Ireland Bucket List Item 39

Attraction: _____

Location: _____

Why I Want To Visit Here: _____

_____

_____

―――― *The Adventure Begins* ――――――――――

Date Of Visit: _____

My Experience: _____

_____

_____

_____

_____

_____

What I Enjoyed Most: _____

_____

_____

The People I Met: _____

_____

_____

Noteworthy

Ireland Bucket List Item **40**

Attraction: _____

Location: _____

Why I Want To Visit Here: _____

_____

_____

————— *The Adventure Begins* —————

Date Of Visit: _____

My Experience: _____

_____

_____

_____

_____

_____

What I Enjoyed Most: _____

_____

_____

The People I Met: _____

_____

_____

41

Noteworthy

Ireland Bucket List Item 41

Attraction: _____

Location: _____

Why I Want To Visit Here: _____

_____

_____

———— *The Adventure Begins* ————

Date Of Visit: _____

My Experience: _____

_____

_____

_____

_____

_____

_____

What I Enjoyed Most: _____

_____

_____

The People I Met: _____

_____

_____

Noteworthy

Ireland Bucket List Item **42**

Attraction: _____

Location: _____

Why I Want To Visit Here: _____

_____

_____

———— *The Adventure Begins* ————————

Date Of Visit: _____

My Experience: _____

_____

_____

_____

_____

_____

_____

What I Enjoyed Most: _____

_____

_____

The People I Met: _____

_____

_____

43

Ireland Bucket List Item 43

Attraction: _____

Location: _____

Why I Want To Visit Here: _____

_____

_____

——— *The Adventure Begins* ———

Date Of Visit: _____

My Experience: _____

_____

_____

_____

_____

_____

_____

What I Enjoyed Most: _____

_____

_____

The People I Met: _____

_____

_____

44

Noteworthy

Ireland Bucket List Item 44

Attraction: _____

Location: _____

Why I Want To Visit Here: _____

_____

_____

——— *The Adventure Begins* ———

Date Of Visit: _____

My Experience: _____

_____

_____

_____

_____

_____

What I Enjoyed Most: _____

_____

_____

The People I Met: _____

_____

_____

45

Noteworthy

Ireland Bucket List Item **45**

Attraction: _____

Location: _____

Why I Want To Visit Here: _____

_____

_____

──────── *The Adventure Begins* ────────

Date Of Visit: _____

My Experience: _____

_____

_____

_____

_____

_____

What I Enjoyed Most: _____

_____

_____

The People I Met: _____

_____

_____

46

Noteworthy

Ireland Bucket List Item 46

Attraction: _____

Location: _____

Why I Want To Visit Here: _____

_____

_____

────── *The Adventure Begins* ──────────

Date Of Visit: _____

My Experience: _____

_____

_____

_____

_____

_____

_____

What I Enjoyed Most: _____

_____

_____

The People I Met: _____

_____

_____

Noteworthy

Ireland Bucket List Item 47

Attraction: _____

Location: _____

Why I Want To Visit Here: _____

_____

_____

———— *The Adventure Begins* ————

Date Of Visit: _____

My Experience: _____

_____

_____

_____

_____

_____

What I Enjoyed Most: _____

_____

_____

The People I Met: _____

_____

_____

48

Ireland Bucket List Item 48

Attraction: _____

Location: _____

Why I Want To Visit Here: _____

_____

_____

───── *The Adventure Begins* ─────

Date Of Visit: _____

My Experience: _____

_____

_____

_____

_____

_____

What I Enjoyed Most: _____

_____

_____

The People I Met: _____

_____

_____

Ireland Bucket List Item **49**

Attraction: _____

Location: _____

Why I Want To Visit Here: _____

_____

_____

──────── *The Adventure Begins* ────────

Date Of Visit: _____

My Experience: _____

_____

_____

_____

_____

_____

What I Enjoyed Most: _____

_____

_____

The People I Met: _____

_____

_____

50

Ireland Bucket List Item 50

Attraction: _____

Location: _____

Why I Want To Visit Here: _____

_____

_____

─── *The Adventure Begins* ───────────────

Date Of Visit: _____

My Experience: _____

_____

_____

_____

_____

_____

What I Enjoyed Most: _____

_____

_____

The People I Met: _____

_____

_____

Adventure Highlights

Adventure Highlights

Adventure Highlights

Adventure Highlights

Adventure Highlights

Adventure Highlights

Adventure Highlights

Adventure Highlights

Adventure Highlights

Adventure Highlights

Adventure Highlights

Adventure Highlights

Adventure Highlights

Made in the USA
Monee, IL
17 January 2020

20458081R00069